Christmas Poems

Chosen by Gaby Morgan

Decorated by Axel Scheffler

MACMILLAN CHILDREN'S BOOKS

To Sue and Peter Morgan –
Happy Christmas from your tallest daughter

First published 2003 by Macmillan Children's Books
This edition published in hardback 2013 by Macmillan Children's Books

Published in paperback 2014 by Macmillan Children's Books
a division of Macmillan Publishers Limited
20 New Wharf Road, London N1 9RR
Basingstoke and Oxford
Associated companies throughout the world
www.panmacmillan.com

ISBN 978-1-4472-5463-8

A CIP catalogue record for this book is available from
the British Library.

Printed in China

Christmas Poems

Gaby Morgan is the Editorial Director for Non-fiction, Poetry and Licensing at Macmillan Children's Books. She has compiled many bestselling anthologies, including *Poems from the First World War*, *Read Me and Laugh: A Funny Poem for Every Day of the Year*, *In My Sky at Twilight: Poems of Eternal Love*, *Fairy Poems* ~ which was shortlisted for the CLPE Award ~ and *A First Poetry Book* with Pie Corbett.

Axel Scheffler enjoys worldwide acclaim for his humorous illustrations. Famous for his many bestselling picture books with Julia Donaldson, including modern classic *The Gruffalo*, Axel is also the illustrator of wonderful novelty and gift books such as the bestselling *The Bedtime Bear* and *Axel Scheffler's Noisy Fa*

Also available from Macmillan Children's Books

The Truth About Christmas
By Philip Ardagh

Christmas Jokes

Contents

Christmas Is Coming

Christmas is coming,
  The geese are getting fat,
Please to put a penny
  In the old man's hat.
If you haven't got a penny,
  A ha'penny will do;
If you haven't got a ha'penny,
  Then God bless you!

Anon.

The Christmas Life

*'If you don't have a real tree, you don't bring the
Christmas life into the house.'*

Josephine Mackinnon, aged 8

Bring in a tree, a young Norwegian spruce,
Bring hyacinths that rooted in the cold.
Bring winter jasmine as its buds unfold –
Bring the Christmas life into this house.

Bring red and green and gold, bring things that
    shine,
Bring candlesticks and music, food and wine.
Bring in your memories of Christmas past.
Bring in your tears for all that you have lost.

Bring in the shepherd boy, the ox and ass,
Bring in the stillness of an icy night,
Bring in a birth, of hope and love and light.
Bring the Christmas life into this house.

Wendy Cope

The Holly and the Ivy

The holly and the ivy,
When they are both full grown,
Of all the trees that are in the wood,
The holly bears the crown.

The rising of the sun
And the running of the deer,
The playing of the merry organ,
Sweet singing in the choir.

The holly bears a blossom
As white as lily flower,
And Mary bore sweet Jesus Christ
To be our sweet Saviour.

The holly bears a berry
As red as any blood,
And Mary bore sweet Jesus Christ
To do poor sinners good.

The holly bears a prickle
As sharp as any thorn,
And Mary bore sweet Jesus Christ
On Christmas Day in the morn.

The holly bears a bark
As bitter as any gall,
And Mary bore sweet Jesus Christ
For to redeem us all.

The holly and the ivy,
When they are both full grown,
Of all the trees that are in the wood,
The holly bears the crown.

Cecil Sharp

Welcome Yule

Now, thrice welcome Christmas,
  Which brings us good cheer,
Minced pies and plum porridge,
  Good ale and strong beer;
With pig, goose, and capon,
  The best that can be,
So well doth the weather
  And our stomachs agree.

Observe how the chimneys
  Do smoke all about,
The cooks are providing
  For dinner no doubt;
But those on whose tables
  No victuals appear,
O may they keep Lent
  All the rest of the year!

With holly and ivy
  So green and so gay,
We deck up our houses
  As fresh as the day.
With bays and rosemary,
  And laurel complete;
And everyone now
  Is a king in conceit.

George Wither

The Angel Gabriel

The angel Gabriel from heaven came,
His wings as drifted snow, his eyes as flame:
'All hail,' said he, 'thou lowly maiden Mary'
Most highly favoured lady! Gloria!

'For known a blessed Mother thou shalt be;
All generations laud and honour thee:
Thy son shall be Emmanuel, by seers foretold'
Most highly favoured lady! Gloria!

~ ‡ ~

Then gentle Mary meekly bowed her head;
'To me be as it pleaseth God!' she said.
'My soul shall laud and magnify his holy Name.'
Most highly favoured lady! Gloria!

Of her Emmanuel, the Christ, was born,
In Bethlehem, all on a Christmas morn;
And Christian folk throughout the world will
    ever say:
Most highly favoured lady! Gloria!

Anon.

Angels

We are made from light.
Called into being we burn
Brighter than the silver white
Of hot magnesium.
More sudden than yellow phosphorous.
We are the fire of heaven;
Blue flames and golden ether.

We are from stars.
Spinning beyond the farthest galaxy
In an instant gathered to this point
We shine, speak our messages and go,
Back to the brilliance.
We are not separate, not individual,
We are what we are made of. Only
Shaped sometimes into tall-winged warriors,
Our faces solemn as swords,
Our voices joy.

The skies are cold;
Suns do not warm us;
Fire does not burn itself.
Only once we touched you
And felt a human heat.
Once, in the brightness of the frost,
Above the hills, in glittering starlight,
Once, we sang.

Jan Dean

from

The Cherry Tree Carol

Joseph was an old man,
　　　And an old man was he,
When he wedded Mary
　　　In the land of Galilee.

When Joseph was married,
　　　And Mary home had got,
Mary proved with child,
　　　By whom Joseph knew not.

Joseph and Mary walked
　　　Through an orchard good,
Where was cherries and berries,
　　　So red as any blood.

Joseph and Mary walked
    Through an orchard green,
Where was berries and cherries
    As thick as might be seen.

O then bespoke Mary,
    So meek and so mild:
'Pluck me one cherry, Joseph,
    For I am with child.'

O then bespoke Joseph,
    With words most unkind:
'Let him pluck thee a cherry
    That brought thee with child.'

O then bespoke the Babe
    Within His mother's womb:
'Bow down then the tallest tree
    For my mother to have some.' $\longrightarrow$

Then bowed down the highest tree
  Unto His mother's hand;
Then she cried: 'See, Joseph,
  I have cherries at command.'

O then bespoke Joseph:
  'I have done Mary wrong;
But cheer up, my dearest,
  And be not cast down.

'O eat your cherries, Mary,
  O eat your cherries now;
O eat your cherries, Mary,
  That grow upon the bough.'

Then Mary plucked a cherry
  As red as the blood;
Then Mary went home
  With her heavy load.

Anon.

Jingle Bells

Dashing through the snow,
In a one-horse open sleigh;
O'er the fields we go,
Laughing all the way;
Bells on bob-tail ring,
Making spirits bright;
Oh what fun to ride and sing
A sleighing song tonight.

Jingle bells, jingle bells,
Jingle all the way;
Oh! What joy it is to ride
In a one-horse open sleigh.
Jingle bells, jingle bells,
Jingle all the way;
Oh! What joy it is to ride
In a one-horse open sleigh.

James Pierpont

A Week to Christmas

Sunday with six whole days to go,
How we'll endure it I don't know!

Monday the goodies are in the making,
Spice smells of pudding and mince pies
   a-baking.

Tuesday, Dad's home late and quiet as a mouse
He smuggles packages into the house.

Wednesday's the day for decorating the tree,
Will the lights work again? We'll have to see.

Thursday's for last-minute shopping and hurry,
We've never seen Mum in quite such a flurry!

Friday is Christmas Eve when we lie awake
Trying to sleep before the daybreak.

And that special quiet on Christmas Morn
When far away in Bethlehem Christ was born.

John Cotton

In the Week When Christmas Comes

This is the week when Christmas comes,
   Let every pudding burst with plums,
And every tree bear dolls and drums,
   In the week when Christmas comes.

Let every hall have boughs of green,
With berries glowing in between,
   In the week when Christmas comes.

Let every doorstep have a song
Sounding the dark street along,
   In the week when Christmas comes.

Let every steeple ring a bell
With a joyful tale to tell,
    In the week when Christmas comes.

Let every night put forth a star
To show us where the heavens are,
    In the week when Christmas comes.

Let every pen enfold a lamb
Sleeping warm beside its dam,
    In the week when Christmas comes.

This is the week when Christmas comes.

Eleanor Farjeon

Deck the Halls

Deck the halls with boughs of holly,
'Tis the season to be jolly,
Don we now our gay apparel,
Troll the ancient Yuletide carol.

See the blazing Yule before us.
Strike the harp and join the chorus,
Follow me in merry measure,
While I tell of Yuletide treasure.

Fast away the old year passes,
Hail the new, ye lads and lasses,
Sing we joyous all together,
Heedless of the wind and weather.

Anon.

The Reverend Sabine Baring-Gould

The Reverend Sabine Baring-Gould,
  Rector (sometime) at Lew,
Once at a Christmas party asked,
  'Whose pretty child are you?'

(The Rector's family was long,
  His memory was poor,
And as to who was who had grown
  Increasingly unsure.)

At this, the infant on the stair
  Most sorrowfully sighed.
'Whose pretty little girl am I?
  'Why, *yours*, Papa!' she cried.

Charles Causley

Wassailers' Carol

Here we come a-wassailing
Among the leaves so green;
Here we come a-wandering
So fair to be seen.

Love and joy to you,
And to you your wassail too,
And God bless you, and send you a
    happy new year,
And God send you a happy new year.

Our wassail cup is made
Of the rosemary tree,
And so is your beer
Of the best barley.

Call up the butler of this house,
Put on his golden ring;
Let him bring us up a glass of beer,
And better shall we sing.

Bring us out a table
And spread it with a cloth;
Bring us out some mouldy cheese,
And some of your Christmas loaf.

God bless the master of this house
Likewise the mistress too,
And all the little children
That round the table go.

Good master and good mistress
While you're sitting by the fire,
Pray think of us poor children
Who are wandering in the mire.

Anon.

Christmas

The bells of waiting Advent ring,
    The Tortoise stove is lit again
And lamp-oil light across the night
    Has caught the streaks of winter rain
In many a stained-glass window sheen
From Crimson Lake to Hooker's Green.

The holly in the windy hedge
    And round the Manor House the yew
Will soon be stripped to deck the ledge,
    The altar, font and arch and pew,
So that the villagers can say
'The church looks nice' on Christmas Day.

Provincial public houses blaze
    And Corporation tramcars clang,
On lighted tenements I gaze
    Where paper decorations hang,
And bunting in the red Town Hall
Says 'Merry Christmas to you all.'

And London shops on Christmas Eve
  Are strung with silver bells and flowers
As hurrying clerks the City leave
  To pigeon-haunted classic towers,
And marbled clouds go scudding by
The many-steepled London sky.

And girls in slacks remember Dad,
  And oafish louts remember Mum,
And sleepless children's hearts are glad,
  And Christmas-morning bells say 'Come!'
Even to shining ones who dwell
Safe in the Dorchester Hotel.

And is it true? And is it true,
  The most tremendous tale of all,
Seen in a stained-glass window's hue,
  A Baby in an ox's stall?
The Maker of the stars and sea
Become a Child on earth for me? $\longrightarrow$

And is it true? For if it is,
   No loving fingers tying strings
Around those tissued fripperies,
   The sweet and silly Christmas things,
Bath salts and inexpensive scent
And hideous tie so kindly meant,

No love that in a family dwells,
   No carolling in frosty air,
Nor all the steeple-shaking bells
   Can with this simple truth compare –
That God was Man in Palestine
And lives today in Bread and Wine.

John Betjeman

Christmas at Four Winds Farm

With the tambourine tinkle of ice on the moor
and the winter moon white as a bone,
my grandad and his father
set out to bring Christmas home.

A wild winter wizard had grizzled the gorse
and spangled the splinter-sharp leaves,
when the light of their wind-swinging lantern
found a magical Christmas tree.

From the glittering town at the end of the dale
the carols grew sweeter and bolder,
as my grandad's smiling father
carried Christmas home on his shoulder.

Maureen Haselhurst

In the Bleak Mid-winter

In the bleak mid-winter
  Frosty wind made moan;
Earth stood hard as iron,
  Water like a stone;
Snow had fallen, snow on snow,
  Snow on snow,
In the bleak mid-winter,
  Long ago.

Our God, heaven cannot hold him
  Nor earth sustain;
Heaven and earth shall flee away
  When he comes to reign:
In the bleak mid-winter
  A stable-place sufficed
The Lord God almighty,
  Jesus Christ.

Angels and archangels
  May have gathered there,
Cherubim and seraphim
  Thronged in the air:
But only his mother
  In her maiden bliss
Worshipped the Beloved
  With a kiss.

What can I give him,
  Poor as I am!
If I were a shepherd
  I would bring a lamb;
If I were a wise man
  I would do my part
Yet what I can I give him –
  Give my heart.

Christina Rossetti

The First Tree in the Greenwood

Now the holly bears a berry as white as the milk,
And Mary bore Jesus, who was wrapped up in silk:
And Mary bore Jesus Christ,
Our Saviour for to be,
And the first tree in the greenwood, it was the
holly.

Now the holly bears a berry as green as the grass,
And Mary bore Jesus, who died on the cross:
And Mary bore Jesus Christ,
Our Saviour for to be,
And the first tree in the greenwood, it was the
holly.

Now the holly bears a berry as black as the coal,
And Mary bore Jesus, who died for us all:
And Mary bore Jesus Christ,
Our Saviour for to be,
And the first tree in the greenwood, it was the
holly.

Now the holly bears a berry, as blood is it red,
Then trust we our Saviour, who rose from the
dead:
And Mary bore Jesus Christ,
Our Saviour for to be,
And the first tree in the greenwood, it was the
holly.

Anon.

Holly Red and Mistletoe White

Holly red and mistletoe white,
The stars are shining with golden light,
Burning like candles this Holy Night,
Holly red and mistletoe white.

Mistletoe white and holly red,
The doors are shut and the children a-bed,
Fairies at foot and angels at head,
Mistletoe white and holly red.

Alison Uttley

Red-berried Holly

Red-berried holly;
Green ivy, pale mistletoe:
Christmas time again.

John Kitching

Tree

a
raw
frost
bites and
winds
rattle my
branches, but
out here is where
I am at home. Yet men
cut me from
my roots, heave
me on trucks away
to the walled prisons
they live in. And there
garla
nded,
in ga
udy f
inery, they sacrif
ice me to a god

Dave Calder

Street Lights

The town leapt a little, tonight,
As the Christmas lights came on.

Everyday streets became more important
And even the darkest pathways glistened.
Stars and snowflakes
Angels and reindeer
Flashed and flickered a holy-white whisper,
Making our town,
Our ordinary, brick and tarmac town,
Sparkle like a frosted castle
In a far-off, frozen land.

Coral Rumble

Just Doing My Job

I'm one of Herod's Henchmen.
We don't have much to say,
We just charge through the audience
In a Henchman sort of way.

We all wear woolly helmets
To hide our hair and ears,
And wellingtons sprayed silver
To match our tinfoil spears.

Our swords are made of cardboard
So blood will not be spilled
If we trip and stab a parent
When the hall's completely filled.

We don't look VERY scary,
We're mostly small and shy,
And some of us wear glasses,
But we give the thing a try.

We whisper Henchman noises
While Herod hunts for strangers,
And then we all charge out again
Like nervous Power Rangers.

Yet when the play is over
And Miss is out of breath
We'll charge like Henchmen through the hall
And scare our mums to death.

Clare Bevan

little tree

little tree
little silent Christmas tree
you are so little
you are more like a flower

who found you in the green forest
and were you very sorry to come away?
see   i will comfort you
because you smell so sweetly

i will kiss your cool bark
and hug you safe and tight
just as your mother would,
only don't be afraid

look   the spangles
that sleep all the year in a dark box
dreaming of being taken out and allowed to
    shine,
the balls the chains red and gold the fluffy
    threads,

put up your little arms
and i'll give them all to you to hold
every finger shall have its ring
and there won't be a single place dark or
    unhappy

then when you're quite dressed
you'll stand in the window for everyone to see
and how they'll stare!
oh but you'll be very proud

and my little sister and i will take hands
and looking up at our beautiful tree
we'll dance and sing
'Noel Noel'

e. e. cummings

forecasts

There are berries this year on the holly.
It wasn't always so.
They may be simply a forecast –
forecast of snow.

There's frost on the sill. I've seen it
glitter with diamond light.
It's slippery, too, the traveller
must watch his step tonight.

There's a moon as big as a melon,
and far-off – O, how far –
flickering on the horizon . . .
a fresh, and different, star . . .

In the heart of man is a coldness.
Through a crack in the stable door
there glimmers a new dominion.

Even ice can thaw.

Jean Kenward

One Christmas Wish?

For snow
to fall all Christmas Eve
in thick, slow flakes;
to fall all through
the hours I drift
in my warm bed
dreaming of Christmas Day.

For snow to lie
next morning
deep and soft;
for me to wake
and see the world
dressed as I've never
seen it dressed
in Christmas white.

For me to plant
my first-time footprints
like a new astronaut
on a new moon;
to snowball, slide,
shout loud 'hallo-oo-oo-s'
through the crisp air;
build snowmen
with red berry lips,
holly green hair.

Later, inside,
to curl up on the rug;
hear grown-ups talk
of snow adventures
Christmases ago.

One wish,
for one white Christmas
– one –
before *I'm* old.

Patricia Leighton

First Snow in the Street

I did not sleep last night.
The falling snow was beautiful and white.
I dressed, sneaked down the stairs
And opened wide the door.
I had not seen such snow before.

Our grubby little street had gone.
The world was brand-new, and everywhere
There was pureness in the air.
I felt such peace. Watching every flake
My heart felt more and more awake.

I thought I'd learned all there was to know
About the trillion million different kinds
Of swirling frosty falling flakes of snow.
But that was not so.
I did not know how vividly it lit
The world with such a peaceful glow.

Upstairs my parents slept,
Yet I could not drag myself away from that sight
To call them down and have them share
The mute miracle that was everywhere.
The snow seemed to fall for me alone.
How beautiful the grubby little street had grown!

Brian Patten

In a Forest Clearing

Pine tree in the forest
Standing tall.
Water dripping from needles
Like crystal baubles –
Exploding on forest floor
Like fairy lights.
Waiting.

Coral Rumble

Snow and Snow

Snow is sometimes a she, a soft one.
    Her kiss on your cheek, her finger on your sleeve
In early December, on a warm evening,
    And you turn to meet her, saying 'It's snowing!'
        But it is not. And nobody's there.
        Empty and calm is the air.

Sometimes the snow is a he, a sly one.
    Weakly he signs the dry stone with a damp spot.
Waifish he floats and touches the pond and is not.
    Treacherous-beggarly he falters, and taps at the
          window.
        A little longer he clings to the grass-blade tip
        Getting his grip. $\longrightarrow$

Then how she leans, how furry foxwrap she
        nestles
    The sky with her warm, and the earth with her
        softness.
How her lit crowding fairytales sink through the
        space-silence
    To build her palace, till it twinkles in starlight –
        Too frail for a foot
        Or a crumb of soot.

Then how his muffled armies move in all night
    And we wake and every road is blockaded
Every hill taken and every farm occupied
    And the white glare of his tents is on the
        ceiling.
        And all that dull blue day and on into the
        gloaming
        We have to watch more coming.

Then everything in the rubbish-heaped world
　　Is a bridesmaid at her miracle.
Dunghills and crumbly dark old barns are bowed
　　　　in the chapel of her sparkle,
　　The gruesome boggy cellars of the wood
　　　　Are a wedding of lace
　　　　Now taking place.

Ted Hughes

Thomas's First Christingle

Thomas is holding
an orange world in his hand
and trying to keep
the candle on top upright.

He touches red ribbon, raisins, nuts
                    – what's it all mean?
'The next bit's magic,'
his sister, Ann, whispers.
'Wait and see!'

In a big circle
all round the pews they stand:
mums, dads, children,
grandparents packed in tight.
One by one the candles are lit
and someone . . .
switches out the church lights!

In the darkness
the Christingle circle glows,
Christ's light
    shining on each single face.

Patricia Leighton

Christmas Market

Tall, white-haired in her widow's black
My Nana took me, balaclava'd from the cold
To where stalls shimmered in a splash of gold,
Buttery light from wind-twitched lamps and all
The Christmas hoards were heaped above my
    eyes,
A shrill cascade of tinsel set to fall
In a sea of shivering colours on the frosty
Foot-pocked earth. I smelt the roasted nuts
Drank syrupy sarsaparilla in thick glasses far
Too hot to hold and chewed a liquorice root
That turned into a soggy yellow brush. The man
Who wound the barrel organ let me turn
The handle and I jangled out a tune –
And Lily of Laguna spangled out into the bright
    night air
And would go on spinning through the turning
    years.

Then we walked home, I clutching a tin car
With half men painted on the windows, chewed a
    sweet
And held her hand as she warmed mine,
One glove lost turning the chattering music.
And I looked up at the circus of the stars
That spread across the city and our street
Coated now with a Christmas cake layer of frost,
And nobody under all those stars I thought
Was a half of a half of a half as happy as me.

Mike Harding

fr xmas' txt msg

where r u? mrsx
lost. frx
where lost? mrsx
fi nu I wunt b lost. frx
nt funny. diner n'ly redi. mrsx
rudolph nose went out in fog. lost. frx
told u it ws goin dim!!! still fogi? mrsx
no – fog gone bt dunt recognise were am now. frx
describe. mrsx
big pointy stone things and camels. frx
u in egypt. mrsx
2morrow I sack rudolph. frx
i give dinner to elves. mrsx
i is sorry. frx
nt haf as sorry as u will be!!! mrsx

Mike Harding

We Are Not Alone

Captain's Log. Starship Saturnalian.
Earth year 2030, day 358 –
The new drive worked! We've tracked the alien
spacecraft that vanished from earth's orbit late

last night. We followed its fantastic leap
across the galaxy and now can see
its sledge-like shape dropping in steep
descent to a planet. Incredibly

a single cosmonaut whose suit glows red
clings to its tail and holds long ropes to steer
a group of prancing creatures: from each head
sprouts aerials that make them look like deer.

The planet's steaming, its surface smooth and
dark as Christmas pudding. Prepare to land!

Dave Calder

Reindeer Report

Chimneys: colder.
Flightpaths: busier.
Driver: Christmas (F)
Still baffled by postcodes.

Children: more
And stay up later.
Presents: heavier
Pay: frozen.

Mission in spite
Of all this
Accomplished.

U. A. Fanthorpe

A Visit from St Nicholas

'Twas the night before Christmas, when all
through the house
Not a creature was stirring, not even a mouse;
The stockings were hung by the chimney with
care,
In hopes that St Nicholas soon would be there;
The children were nestled all snug in their beds,
While visions of sugar-plums danced in their
heads;
And mamma in her 'kerchief, and I in my cap,
Had just settled our brains for a long winter's nap –
When out on the lawn there arose such a clatter,
I sprang from my bed to see what was the matter.
Away to the window I flew like a flash,
Tore open the shutters, and threw up the sash.
The moon, on the breast of the new-fallen snow,
Gave the lustre of midday to objects below;
When, what to my wondering eyes should appear,
But a miniature sleigh and eight tiny reindeer, →

With a little old driver, so lively and quick,
I knew in a moment it must be St Nick.
More rapid than eagles his coursers they came,
And he whistled, and shouted, and called them by
    name:
'Now, *Dasher*! now, *Dancer*! now, *Prancer* and
    Vixen!
On, *Comet*! on, *Cupid*! on, *Donder* and *Blitzen*!

To the top of the porch! to the top of the wall!
Now dash away! dash away! dash away all!'
As dry leaves that before the wild hurricane fly,
When they meet with an obstacle, mount to the
    sky;
So up to the house-top the coursers they flew
With the sleigh full of toys, and St Nicholas too.
And then, in a twinkling, I heard on the roof
The prancing and pawing of each little hoof –
As I drew in my head, and was turning around,
Down the chimney St Nicholas came with a
    bound.
He was dressed all in fur, from his head to his
    foot,

And his clothes were all tarnished with ashes and
    soot;
A bundle of toys he had flung on his back,
And he looked like a pedlar just opening his pack.
His eyes – how they twinkled; his dimples, how
    merry!
His cheeks were like roses, his nose like a cherry!
His droll little mouth was drawn up like a bow,
And the beard of his chin was as white as the
    snow;
The stump of a pipe he held tight in his teeth,
And the smoke it encircled his head like a wreath;
He had a broad face and a little round belly
That shook, when he laughed, like a bowl full of
    jelly.
He was chubby and plump, a right jolly old elf,
And I laughed when I saw him, in spite of myself;
A wink of his eye and a twist of his head
Soon gave me to know I had nothing to dread;
He spoke not a word, but went straight to his
    work, $\longrightarrow$

And filled all the stockings; then turned with a
    jerk,
And laying his fingers aside of his nose,
And giving a nod, up the chimney he rose;
He sprang to his sleigh, to his team gave a whistle,
And away they all flew like the down of a thistle.
But I heard him exclaim, ere he drove out of sight,
'Happy Christmas to all, and to all a good night!'

Clement Clarke Moore

Christmas Eve

Our
pud is
cooked,
meat stuffed and rolled –
smells drift of fruit and almonds where
the cake is iced and waiting.

Our tree is up, green, red and gold,
and twists of tinsel shimmer there
from lights illuminating.

Our foil-wrapped secrets to unfold,
and tiptoe stockings hung with care,
are all at once creating

A feeling that we want to hold
suspended in the tingling air –
It's
called
anticipating.

Liz Brownlee

Christmas Eve

On Christmas Eve
it is so late
that even Mum and Dad
are fast asleep in bed

I stand at the top of the stairs.

The house is warm
and the tree lights glow.

I can smell mince pies
and anticipation.

I make a wish.

Roger Stevens

The Christmas Eve News

Good evening.

The police authorities are hopeful that tonight they will finally get to the bottom of their longest-standing unsolved mystery – the case of the serial present-giver Father Christmas, also known as Santa Claus.

Inspector Hunch of Scotland Yard said that the police have, with the help of an advanced computer program, found a pattern to the break-ins by this intruder and are confident that he will strike again tonight.

Inspector Hunch went on to add that members of the public should not be unduly alarmed by the likelihood of a break-in and stressed that although the strange intruder always leaves gifts he has never been known to take anything other than the odd mince pie and a tipple from the liquor cabinet. $\longrightarrow$

To assist the police with this investigation, in shopping centres all over the country, reconstructions have been staged with the help of Father Christmas look-alikes performing the act of giving. It is hoped that these reconstructions might jog the memories of members of the public with any information which might help unmask the mystery giver.

Father Christmas is described as tallish, heavily bearded and athletic though overweight. He is said to dress in a red suit and matching bobble hat. The police advise members of the public who witness Father Christmas in the act of leaving presents in their bedrooms to pretend to be asleep but urged them to phone Scotland Yard as soon as the intruder has left the scene of the generosity.

Now the Christmas Eve weather. Under tonight's brightly shining moon, deep snow is expected of the crisp and even kind. A cruel frost is expected later.

That is the end of the news.

Wishing you all a safe and a Merry Christmas.

Goodnight.

Philip Waddell

Wanted

WANTED a reliable STAR
to lead a small party westwards.
Bright with good sense of direction.
No timewasters.
Send CV to CHILDTREK,
EARTH.

Sue Cowling

Love Came Down at Christmas

Love came down at Christmas,
  Love all lovely, Love Divine;
Love was born at Christmas,
  Star and angels gave the sign.

Worship we the Godhead,
  Love Incarnate, Love Divine;
Worship we our Jesus:
  But wherewith for sacred sign?

Love shall be our token,
  Love be yours and love be mine,
Love to God and all men,
  Love for plea and gift and sign.

Christina Rossetti

Little Donkey

Little donkey, what did you do,
what did you do on Christmas Eve?
'I carried a woman, her head bowed down.
I carried her into Bethlehem town.'

Little donkey, what did you hear,
what did you hear on Christmas Night?
'I heard the angels, the sky was torn
as they sang out joyfully, "Christ is born."'

Little donkey, who were you with,
who were you with on Christmas Night?
'I was with the ox who stood quite still
as the shepherds ran from the star-bright hills.'

Little donkey, what did you see,
what did you see on Christmas Day?
'I saw a Babe in a manger bed,
a heavenly light about His head.'

Little donkey, who followed the Star,
who followed the Star on Christmas Night?
'Three kings of splendour and of pride
who fell to their knees at the Baby's side.'

Little donkey, what do you bear,
what do you bear to remember Him?
'I bear the Cross, the Cross on my back,
etched in velvety brown and black.
I bear the Cross to remember Him.'

Marian Swinger

Mary's Burden

My Baby, my Burden,
    To-morrow the morn
I shall go lighter
    And you will be born.

I shall go lighter,
    But heavier too
For seeing the burden
    That falls upon you.

The burden of love,
    The burden of pain,
I'll see you bear both
    Among men once again.

To-morrow you'll bear it
  Your burden alone,
To-night you've no burden
  That is not my own.

My Baby, my Burden,
  To-morrow the morn
I shall go lighter
  And you will be born.

Eleanor Farjeon

O little Town of Bethlehem

O little town of Bethlehem
　　How still we see thee lie!
Above thy deep and dreamless sleep
　　The silent stars go by.

Yet in thy dark streets shineth
　　The everlasting light,
The hopes and fears of all the years
　　Are met in thee tonight.

O morning stars, together
　　Proclaim the holy birth,
And praises sing to God the King,
　　And peace to men on earth;
For Christ is born of Mary;
　　And, gathered all above,
While mortals sleep, the angels keep
　　Their watch of wondering love.

How silently, how silently,
  The wondrous gift is given!
So God imparts to human hearts
  The blessings of his heaven.
No ear may hear his coming;
  But in this world of sin,
Where meek souls will receive him, still
  The dear Christ enters in.

 O holy Child of Bethlehem
  Descend to us we pray;
Cast out our sin, and enter in,
  Be born in us today.
We hear the Christmas angels
  The great glad tidings tell:
A come to us, abide with us;
  Our Lord Emmanuel.

Bishop Phillips Brooks

Saturday Night at the Bethlehem Arms

Very quiet really for a Saturday.
Just the old couple come to visit relations
Who took the double room above the yard
And were both of them in bed by half past nine.
Left me with that other one, the stranger.
Sat like he was set till Domesday at the corner of
    the bar
Sipping small beer dead slow and keeping mum,
Those beady tax-collector's eyes of his
On my reflection in the glass behind the bar
Watching me, watching me.
And when he did get round to saying something
His talk was like those lines of gossamer
That fishermen send whispering across the water
To lure and hook unwary fish.
Not my type. And anyway I'd been on the go since
    five.
Dead beat I was.

Some of us have a bed to go to, I thought to
    myself.
I was just about to call Time
When the knock came at the door.
At first I was for turning them away;
We only have two rooms see and both of them
    were taken.
But something desperate in the woman's eyes
Made me think again and I told them,
They could rough it in the barn
If they didn't mind the cows and mules for
    company.
I know, I know. Soft, that's me.

I yawned, locked up, turned out the lights,
Rinsed my hands to lose the smell of beer.
Went up to bed.
A day like any other.
That's how it is.
Nothing much ever happens here.

Gareth Owen

The Innkeeper of Bethlehem

'There's no room at the inn,' he told them.
'We're full up, I am sorry to say.
Inn's crammed with people. Can't help it.
I'm having to turn folk away.'
But there was something about the young
    woman
and the innkeeper shouted out, 'Wait.
I suppose you could sleep in the stable,
there's nothing else left, and it's late.'
He showed them both round to the stable
and settled them down for the night,
then he left, glancing up at the heavens
where a star shone unnaturally bright,
gilding his face with a splendour
that no one on earth ever saw
as he entered his inn, slightly dazzled,
quietly closing the door.

Marian Swinger

Nativity

Holly and ivy and mistletoe green
Bow to the lady who is our Lord's queen.

Bright silver stars in the sky high above
Shine on the boy-child who brings us his love.

Angels who pattern the heavens with your wings
Sing to the Christ-child, the king of all kings.

Shepherds who reason not why but just come
Teach us your faith in God's holy Son.

White dove of Peace riding the storm
Feather his fears and keep his soul warm. $\longrightarrow$

Watch by his manger brown robin and weep
For the harvest of sins which his sweet blood will
   reap.

Mary, O Mary, take comfort from all
For the hope of the world is asleep in this stall.

Patricia Leighton

Listen

Listen.
Far away, the snort of a camel,
The swish of boots in the endless sand,
The whisper of silk and the clatter of
ceremonial swords,
Far away.

Listen.
Not so far, the slam of a castle door,
A cry of rage on the midnight air,
A jangle of spurs and the cold thrust of a
soldier's command,
Not so far.

Listen.
Closer now, the homely bleat of a ewe among
the grasses,
The answering call of her lamb, fresh born,
The rattle of stones on a hillside path,
Closer now. $\longrightarrow$

Listen.
Closer still, the murmur of women in the dark,
The kindly creak of a stable door,
The steady breathing of the sleepy beasts,
Closer still.

Listen.
So close you are almost there,
The singing of the stars,
The soundless flurry of wings,
The soft whimper of a child amongst the straw,
So close you are almost there.

Clare Bevan

It Came Upon the Midnight Clear

It came upon the midnight clear,
  That glorious song of old,
From angels bending near the earth
  To touch their harps of gold:
'Peace on the earth, good will to men,
  From heaven's all-gracious King!'
The world in solemn stillness lay
  To hear the angels sing.

Still through the cloven skies they come,
  With peaceful wings unfurled;
And still their heavenly music floats
  O'er all the weary world:
Above its sad and lowly plains
  They bend on hovering wing;
And ever o'er its Babel-sounds
  The blessed angels sing. $\longrightarrow$

Yet with the woes of sin and strife
  The world has suffered long;
Beneath the angel-strain have rolled
  Two thousand years of wrong;
And man, at war with man, hears not
  The love-song which they bring:
O hush the noise, ye men of strife,
  And hear the angels sing.

For lo, the days are hastening on,
  By prophet-bards foretold,
When, with the ever-circling years,
  Comes round the age of gold;
When peace shall over all the earth
  Its ancient splendours fling,
And the whole world give back the song
  Which now the angels sing.

Edmund Hamilton Sears

Before the Paling of the Stars

Before the paling of the stars,
 Before the winter morn,
 Before the earliest cock-crow,
 Jesus Christ was born:
  Born in a stable,
 Cradled in a manger,
In the world his hands had made
 Born a stranger.

Priest and King lay fast asleep
 In Jerusalem;
Young and old lay fast asleep
 In crowded Bethlehem;
Saint and Angel, ox and ass,
 Kept a watch together,
 Before the Christmas daybreak
 In the winter weather. $\longrightarrow$

Jesus on His Mother's breast
    In the stable cold,
Spotless Lamb of God was He,
    Shepherd of the fold:
Let us kneel with Mary Maid
    With Joseph bent and hoary,
With Saint and Angel, ox and ass,
    To hail the King of Glory.

Christina Rossetti

Nativity

When God decided to be bones and skin and
    blood like us
He didn't choose a palace, nothing grand – no
    frills and fuss.
He slipped in through the back door, with the
    straw and hay and dust.
He just became a baby with no choice but to trust.
And love us without question, as every baby must.

But Creation knew the wonder of this tiny
    newborn King.
The crystal depths of space were touched, the air
    itself would sing.
The Word is flesh. The silence of the glittering
    stars is shattered. Heaven rings.
The sky blazed wild with angels, whose song was
    fire and snow.
When God lay in his mother's arms two thousand
    years ago.

Jan Dean

from
Past Three O'Clock

Past three o'clock
And a cold frosty morning:
Past three o'clock:
Good morrow, masters all!

Born is a Baby
Gentle as may be,
Son of th' eternal
Father supernal.

Seraph quire singeth,
Angel bell ringeth,
Hark how they rime it,
Time it and chime it!

Mid earth rejoices
Hearing such voices
Ne'ertofore so well
Carolling 'Nowell'.

George Ratcliffe Woodward

The Rocking Carol

Little Jesus, sweetly sleep, do not stir;
We will lend a coat of fur,
　　We will rock you, rock you, rock you,
　　We will rock you, rock you, rock you:
See the fur to keep you warm
Snugly round your tiny form.

Mary's little baby, sleep, sweetly sleep,
Sleep in comfort, slumber deep,
　　We will rock you, rock you, rock you,
　　We will rock you, rock you, rock you:
We will serve you all we can,
Darling, darling little man.

Percy Dearmer

Mary's Song

Sleep, King Jesus,
Your royal bed
Is made of hay
In a cattle-shed.
Sleep, King Jesus,
Do not fear,
Joseph is watching
And waiting near.

Warm in the wintry air
You lie,
The ox and the donkey
Standing by,
With summer eyes
They seem to say:
Welcome, Jesus,
On Christmas Day!

Sleep, King Jesus:
Your diamond crown
High in the sky
Where the stars look down.
Let your reign
Of love begin,
That all the world
May enter in.

Charles Causley

A Cradle Song

Sweet dreams form a shade
O'er my lovely infant's head:
Sweet dreams of pleasant streams
By happy, silent moony beams.

Sweet sleep with soft down
Weave thy brows an infant crown;
Sweet sleep, angel mild,
Hover o'er my happy child.

Sweet smiles in the night,
Hover over my delight;
Sweet smiles, mother's smiles,
All the livelong night beguiles.

Sweet moans, dovelike sighs,
Chase not slumber from thy eyes;
Sweet moans, sweeter smiles,
All the dovelike moans beguiles.

Sleep, sleep, happy child;
All creation slept and smiled;
Sleep, sleep, happy sleep,
While o'er thee thy mother weep.

Sweet babe, in thy face
Holy image I can trace:
Sweet babe, once like thee
Thy Maker lay and wept for me.

Wept for me, for thee, for all
When He was an infant small:
Thou His image ever see,
Heavenly face that smiles on thee.

Smiles on me, on thee, on all,
Who became an infant small:
Infant smiles are His own smiles,
Heaven and earth to peace beguiles.

William Blake

Christmas Morn

Shall I tell you what will come
to Bethlehem on Christmas morn,
who will kneel them gently down
before the Lord new-born?

One small fish from the river,
with scales of red, red gold,
one wild bee from the heather,
one grey lamb from the fold,
one ox from the high pasture,
one black bull from the herd,
one goatling from the far hills,
one white, white bird.

And many children – God give them grace,
bringing tall candles to light Mary's face.

Ruth Sawyer

The Coventry Carol

Lully, lullay, thou little tiny child,
By by, lully, lullay, thou little tiny child,
By by, lully, lullay,

O sisters too, how may we do
For to preserve this day
This poor youngling for whom we do sing,
By by, lully lullay?

Herod the king, in his raging,
Charged he hath this day
His men of might, in his own sight,
All young children to slay.

Then woe is me, poor child for thee!
And ever mourn and say,
For thy parting neither say nor sing
By by, lully, lullay.

Anon.

Robin

In the stable where the Christ child lay
A small brown bird pecked in the hay,
The stable's fire was almost dead
And seeing this, the small bird spread
Its wings out by the last faint spark.
Then, fluttering like a meadowlark,
It fanned it once more into flame.
Good Joseph built the fire again.
Mary, smiling, blessed the bird.
Neither she nor Joseph heard
The bird's faint cries, and neither guessed
At the burnt feathers on its breast.

But when in God's good time new feathers came,
The robin's breast was red as any flame.

Eric Finney

What the Donkey Saw

No room in the inn, of course,
And not that much in the stable,
What with the shepherds, Magi, Mary,
Joseph, the heavenly host –
Not to mention the baby
Using our manger as a cot.
You couldn't have squeezed another cherub in
For love or money.

Still, in spite of the overcrowding,
I did my best to make them feel wanted.
I could see the baby and I
Would be going places together.

U. A. Fanthorpe

While Shepherds Watched Their Flocks

While shepherds watched their flocks by
    night,
All seated on the ground,
The angel of the Lord came down,
And glory shone around.

'Fear not,' said he (for mighty dread
Had seized their troubled mind);
'Glad tidings of great joy I bring
To you and all mankind.

'To you in David's town this day
Is born of David's line
A Saviour, who is Christ the Lord;
And this shall be the sign:

'The heavenly Babe you there shall find
To human view displayed,
All meanly wrapped in swathing bands,
And in a manger laid.'

Thus spake the seraph; and forthwith
Appeared a shining throng
Of angels praising God, who thus
Addressed their joyful song:

'All glory be to God on high,
And to the earth be peace;
Good will henceforth from heaven to men
Begin and never cease.'

Nahum Tate

The First Christmas

It never snows at Christmas
in that dry and dusty land.
Instead of freezing blizzards,
there are palms and drifting sands
and years ago, a stable
and above, a glorious star
and three wise men who followed it
on camels, from afar,
while, sleepy on the quiet hills,
a shepherd gave a cry.
He'd seen a crowd of angels
in the silent, starlit sky.
In the stable, ox and ass stood
very still and calm,
gazing at the baby
safe and snug in Mary's arms.

But Joseph, lost in shadow,
face lit by an oil lamp's glow,
stood wondering, that first Christmas day,
two thousand years ago.

Marian Swinger

Welcome to Heaven's King

Welcome to Thou, Heaven's King,
Welcome, born in one morning,
Welcome, for Him we shall sing,
    Welcome, Yule!

Anon.

Hymn for Christmas Day

Christians awake, salute the happy morn,
Whereon the Saviour of the world was born;
Rise, to adore the mystery of love,
Which hosts of angels chanted from above:
With them the joyful tidings first begun
Of God incarnate, and the Virgin's son.
Then to the watchful shepherds it was told,
Who heard the angelic herald's voice: 'Behold!
I bring good tidings of a Saviour's birth,
To you, and all the nations upon earth!
This day hath God fulfilled his promised Word;
This day is born a Saviour, Christ, the Lord.
In David's city, shepherds, ye shall find
The long foretold redeemer of mankind;
Wrapped up in swaddling clothes, the babe divine
Lies in a manger: this shall be your sign.'
He spake, and straightway the celestial choir,
In hymns of joy unknown before, conspire:
The praises of redeeming love they sung,
And heaven's whole orb with hallelujahs rung. $\longrightarrow$

God's highest glory was their anthem still;
Peace upon earth and mutual good will.
To Bethlehem straight the enlightened shepherds
    ran,
To see the wonder God had wrought for man;
And found, with Joseph and the blessed maid,
Her Son, the Saviour, in a manger laid.
Amazed, the wondrous story they proclaim –
The first apostles of His infant fame:
While Mary keeps, and ponders in her heart,
The heavenly vision which the swains impart.
They to their flocks, still praising God, return,
And their glad hearts within their bosoms burn.

    Let us, like these good shepherds then, employ
Our grateful voices to proclaim the joy:
Like Mary, let us ponder in our mind
God's wondrous love in saving lost mankind;
Artless and watchful as these favoured swains,
While virgin meekness in the heart remains:
Trace we the babe, who has retrieved our loss,
From His poor manger to His bitter cross;
Treading His steps, assisted by His grace,
Till man's first heavenly state again takes place.

Then may we hope the angelic thrones among
To sing, redeemed, a glad triumphal song.
He that was born upon this joyful day
Around us all His glory shall display;
Saved by His love, incessant we shall sing
Of angels, and of angel-men, the King.

John Byrom

Bells Ringing

I heard bells ringing
Suddenly all together, one wild, intricate figure,
A mixture of wonder and praise
Climbing the winter-winged air in December.
Norwich, Gloucester, Salisbury, combined with
  York
To shake Worcester and Paul's into the old
  discovery
Made frost-fresh again.
I heard these rocketing and wound-remembering
  chimes
Running their blessed counterpoint
Round the mazes of my mind,
And felt their message brimming over with love,
Watering my cold heart,
Until, as over all England hundreds of towers
  trembled

Beneath the force of Christmas rolling out,
I knew, as shepherds and magi knew,
That all sounds had been turned into one sound,
And a single golden bell,
Repeating, as knees bowed, the name
    EMMANUEL.

Leonard Clark

We Wish You a Merry Christmas

We wish you a merry Christmas,
We wish you a merry Christmas,
We wish you a merry Christmas,
And a happy New Year.

Good tidings we bring
To you and your kin,
We wish you a merry Christmas,
And a happy New Year.

Now bring us some figgy pudding,
Now bring us some figgy pudding,
Now bring us some figgy pudding,
And bring some out here.
Chorus

For we all like figgy pudding,
For we all like figgy pudding,
For we all like figgy pudding,
So bring some out here.
Chorus

And we won't go until we've had some,
And we won't go until we've had some,
And we won't go until we've had some,
So bring some out here.
Chorus

Anon.

Christmas Morning

early on
everything frosted like iron
we woke, my brother and I,
to the creak on the stair
and silently
pumped like balloons
with excitement
we pretended sleep
until Santa (or Mum or Dad)
had gone –

ducked our heads into Christmas
pillow sacks of –

crackly paper
oranges and apples sweet and tangy
chocolate money
plastic made-in-Hong Kong rockets
sheriff's badge
pair of socks (from Auntie May, hand
    knitted)
a colouring book
and pencils that smell of Friday afternoons
    in school
a bag of dinosaurs, red, blue, brown and
    green
a false nose
a set of magic tricks
a crêpe paper cracker with glossy band
a rattly handful of walnuts at the bottom
a thread of cotton
a few sparks of glitter . . .

I wish I could live inside here
for ever!

Stephen Bowkett

Christmas Stocking

What will go into the Christmas Stocking
While the clock on the mantelpiece goes
   tick-tocking?

An orange, a penny,
Some sweets, not too many,
A trumpet, a dolly,
A sprig of red holly,
A book and a top
And a grocery shop,
Some beads in a box,
An ass and an ox
And a lamb, plain and good,
All whittled in wood,
A white sugar dove,
A handful of love,
Another of fun,
And it's very near done –
A big silver star
On top – there you are!

Come morning you'll wake to the clock's
    tick-tocking,
And that's what you'll find in the Christmas
    Stocking.

Eleanor Farjeon

Stocking

The old long stockings – every year
their thick brown weave was stuffed
into stiffness, stretched
like a cartoon ostrich neck
with knobbly shapes – the parcels
to be teased out one by one with that intense
all-involving mix of hope and dread –
for who thinks on the past or future in
the moment of unwrapping the present?

So, every year, starting with
the largest lumps stuck in the stocking's throat,
we'd work our way down, tunnelling
to find if fate matched our desires –
so difficult at seven in the morning
to praise the unwanted or expected,
to mask disappointment at the not quite right:

but life itself is a gift, even if it's
not just what we wanted,
and from gifts we learn to accept,
to understand at last that the real gift
was the stocking itself, year after year,
and the hands that filled it, and the certainty
that after everything or anything,
however hollow our fantasies proved,
we would always find, tucked in the toe
a tangerine, an apple,
and a sixpence.

Dave Calder

I Saw Three Ships Come Sailing In

I saw three ships come sailing in,
On Christmas Day, on Christmas Day,
I saw three ships come sailing in,
On Christmas Day in the morning.

And what was in those ships all three?
On Christmas Day, on Christmas Day,
And what was in those ships all three?
On Christmas Day in the morning.

Our Saviour Christ and his lady,
On Christmas Day, on Christmas Day,
Our Saviour Christ and his lady,
On Christmas Day in the morning.

O they sailed into Bethlehem,
On Christmas Day, on Christmas Day,
O they sailed into Bethlehem,
On Christmas Day in the morning.

And all the bells on earth shall ring,
On Christmas Day, on Christmas Day,
And all the bells on earth shall ring,
On Christmas Day in the morning.

And all the angels in heaven shall sing,
On Christmas Day, on Christmas Day,
And all the angels in heaven shall sing,
On Christmas Day in the morning.

And all the souls on earth shall sing,
On Christmas Day, on Christmas Day,
And all the souls on earth shall sing,
On Christmas Day in the morning.

Then let us all rejoice amain!
On Christmas Day, on Christmas Day,
Then let us all rejoice amain!
On Christmas Day in the morning.

Anon.

A Christmas Blessing

God bless the master of this house,
  The mistress also,
And all the little children
  That round the table go;
And all your kin and kinsfolk
  That dwell both far and near:
I wish you a Merry Christmas
  And a Happy New Year.

Anon.

As I Sat on a Sunny Bank

As I sat on a sunny bank
On Christmas day in the morning,
I saw three ships come sailing by
On Christmas day in the morning.
And who do you think were in those ships
But Joseph and his fair lady:
He did whistle and she did sing,
And all the bells on earth did ring
For joy our Saviour He was born
On Christmas day in the morning.

Anon.

A Martian Christmas

After a long year and a half in space,
We reached Mars –
December 25th, 2033!
Christmas dinner was all planned –
Freeze-dried turkey and roast potatoes,
With Christmas pud squeezed from a tube to
    follow.
Presents were a problem –
We hadn't been able to stop off
For shopping on the way.

And we went outside for the first time,
And got depressed.
Sand, nothing but sand.
'Maybe the three wise men
Will come plodding round that sand dune
On their camels,'
Someone said, but we didn't laugh.
We were too busy thinking about Christmas,
But that was fifty million miles away.

Then we saw the star,
Hanging like a lantern in the east.
'It's Earth,' someone said.
We just looked and looked –
It must have been the brightness of it
That made our eyes water.

David Orme

It Was on Christmas Day

It was on Christmas Day,
And all in the morning,
Our Saviour was born,
And our heavenly King:
And was not this a joyful thing?
And sweet Jesus they called him by name.

Anon.

The Christmas Shed

It was late afternoon on Christmas Day
with light fading and flakes falling
when the three of us raced through the copse
where rhododendrons and holly bushes
bent low under their burden of fresh snow.
Gasping, we skidded to a stop
at the edge of the estate's allotments.
A bitter, whining wind made us shiver
as it whipped across the frozen earth.
    'No one's about. Come on!'

Slipping and skating we dashed to Jacko's shed
and at the back crawled in through a hole
where the old boards had rotted away.
Inside it was dry. The air was still.
We peered as daylight filtered dimly
through the fly-spattered, cobwebby window,
and breathed the shed's special smell
of pine, creosote, paraffin and sawdust.
Fear of discovery made us whisper.
    'Let's see if they're there.' $\longrightarrow$

Carefully we moved garden implements
that were stacked in a corner.
Dried soil fell and crunched beneath our boots
as we shifted rakes, forks, spades and hoes,
and there was Smoky and her four kittens
warm in a bed of worn gloves and jerseys.
Like the Three Kings we knelt and offered
our Christmas gifts – turkey scraps, ham, a
　　sausage.
Smoky arched and purred and ate hungrily.
　'The kittens are still blind.'

The food vanished. We watched in silence
as the grey cat lay down and her mewling kittens
guzzled greedily at the milk bar.
    'It's late.' We replaced the implements
and crept out of Jacko's old shed.
Like shadows we hared for the cover of the copse.
Now the snow was heavy. Day's last light was
    dying.
Chilled to the bone we reached our estate
where Christmas lights were flashing. We split.
    'Same time tomorrow?'
        'Yeah.'
            'See you.'

Wes Magee

The Twelve Days of Christmas

On the first day of Christmas
My true love sent to me,
A partridge in a pear tree.

On the second day of Christmas
My true love sent to me,
Two turtle doves,
And a partridge in a pear tree.

On the third day of Christmas
My true love sent to me,
Three French hens, two turtle doves,
And a partridge in a pear tree.

On the fourth day of Christmas
My true love sent to me,
Four calling birds, three French hens,
Two turtle doves, and a partridge in a pear
    tree.

On the fifth day of Christmas
My true love sent to me,
Five gold rings, four calling birds,
Three French hens, two turtle doves,
And a partridge in a pear tree.

On the sixth day of Christmas
My true love sent to me,
Six geese a-laying, five gold rings,
Four calling birds, three French hens,
Two turtle doves, and a partridge in a pear
    tree.

On the seventh day of Christmas
My true love sent to me,
Seven swans a-swimming, six geese a-laying,
Five gold rings, four calling birds,
Three French hens, two turtle doves,
And a partridge in a pear tree. $\longrightarrow$

On the eighth day of Christmas
My true love sent to me,
Eight maids a-milking, seven swans
    a-swimming,
Six geese a-laying, five gold rings,
Four calling birds, three French hens,
Two turtle doves, and a partridge in a pear
    tree.

On the ninth day of Christmas
My true love sent to me,
Nine drummers drumming, eight maids
    a-milking,
Seven swans a-swimming, six geese a-laying,
Five gold rings, four calling birds,
Three French hens, two turtle doves,
And a partridge in a pear tree.

On the tenth day of Christmas
My true love sent to me,
Ten pipers piping, nine drummers
    drumming,
Eight maids a-milking, seven swans
    a-swimming,
Six geese a-laying, five gold rings,
Four calling birds, three French hens,
Two turtle doves, and a partridge in a pear
    tree.

On the eleventh day of Christmas
My true love sent to me,
Eleven ladies dancing, ten pipers piping,
Nine drummers drumming, eight maids
    a-milking,
Seven swans a-swimming, six geese a-laying,
Five gold rings, four calling birds,
Three French hens, two turtle doves,
And a partridge in a pear tree. ⟶

On the twelfth day of Christmas
My true love sent to me,
Twelve lords a-leaping,
Eleven ladies dancing,
Ten pipers piping,
Nine drummers drumming,
Eight maids a-milking,
Seven swans a-swimming,
Six geese a-laying,
Five gold rings,
Four calling birds,
Three French hens,
Two turtle doves,
And a partridge in a pear tree.

Anon.

On the Thirteenth Day of Christmas My True Love Phoned Me Up . . .

Well, I suppose I should be grateful, you've obviously gone
to a lot of trouble and expense – or maybe off your head.
Yes, I did like the birds – the small ones anyway were fun
if rather messy, but now the hens have roosted on my bed
and the rest are nested on the wardrobe. It's hard to sleep
with all that cooing, let alone the cackling of the geese $\longrightarrow$

whose eggs are everywhere, but mostly in a
      broken smelly heap
on the sofa. No, why should I mind? I can't get
      any peace
anywhere – the lounge is full of drummers
      thumping tom-toms
and sprawling lords crashed out from manic
      leaping. The kitchen
is crammed with cows and milkmaids and
      smells of a million stink-bombs
and enough sour milk to last a year. The
      pipers? I'd forgotten them –
they were no trouble, I paid them and they
      went. But I can't get rid
of these young ladies. They won't stop dancing
      or turn the music down

and they're always in the bathroom, squealing
   as they skid
across the flooded floor. No, I don't need a
   plumber round,
it's just the swans – where else can they swim?
   Poor things,
I think they're going mad, like me. When I
   went to wash my
hands one ate the soap, another swallowed
   the gold rings.
And the pear tree died. Too dry. So thanks for
   nothing, love. Goodbye.

Dave Calder

We Three Kings of Orient Are

We three kings of Orient are;
Bearing gifts we traverse afar,
Field and fountain, moor and mountain,
Following yonder star:

    O star of wonder, star of night,
    Star with royal beauty bright,
    Westward leading, still proceeding,
    Guide us to thy perfect light.

Born a king on Bethlehem's plain,
Gold I bring, to crown him again,
King for ever, ceasing never
Over us all to reign:

Frankincense to offer have I,
Incense owns a deity nigh;
Prayer and praising, all men raising,
Worship him, God most high:

Myrrh is mine; its bitter perfume
Breathes a life of gathering gloom;
Sorrowing, sighing, bleeding, dying,
Sealed in the stone-cold tomb:

Glorious now behold him arise,
King and God and sacrifice,
Heaven sings 'Alleluya',
'Alleluya' the earth replies:

John Henry Hopkins

Bright Star

(A Haiku)

Bright star studs night sky.
Three Wise Men gaze up amazed,
And follow, like children, thrilled.

John Kitching

Journey of the Magi

'A cold coming we had of it,
Just the worst time of the year
For a journey, and such a long journey:
The ways deep and the weather sharp,
The very dead of winter.'
And the camels galled, sore-footed, refractory,
Lying down in the melting snow.
There were times we regretted
The summer palaces on slopes, the terraces,
And the silken girls bringing sherbet.
Then the camel men cursing and grumbling
And running away, and wanting their liquor and
     women,
And the night-fires going out, and the lack of
     shelters,
And the cities hostile and the towns unfriendly
And the villages dirty and charging high prices:
A hard time we had of it.
At the end we preferred to travel all night,
Sleeping in snatches, $\longrightarrow$

With the voices singing in our ears, saying
That this was all folly.
Then at dawn we came down to a temperate
    valley,
Wet, below the snow-line, smelling of vegetation;
With a running stream and a water-mill beating
    the darkness,
And three trees on the low sky,
And an old white horse galloped away in the
    meadow.
Then we came to a tavern with vine-leaves over
    the lintel,
Six hands at an open door dicing for pieces of
    silver,
And feet kicking the empty wineskins.
But there was no information, and so we
    continued
And arrived at evening, not a moment too soon
Finding the place; it was (you may say)
    satisfactory.
All this was a long time ago, I remember,
And I would do it again, but set down
This set down

This: were we led all that way for
Birth or Death? There was a Birth, certainly,
We had evidence and no doubt.
I had seen birth and death,
But had thought they were different; this Birth
  was
Hard and bitter agony for us, like Death, our
  death.
We returned to our places, these kingdoms,
But no longer at ease here, in the old
  dispensation,
With an alien people clutching their gods.
I should be glad of another death.

T. S. Eliot

The Meeting Place

(after Rubens: The Adoration
of the Magi, 1634)

It was the arrival of the kings
that caught us unawares;
we'd looked in on the woman in the barn,
curiosity you could call it,
something to do on a cold winter's night;
we'd wished her well –
that was the best we could do, she was in pain,
and the next thing we knew
she was lying on the straw
– the little there was of it –
and there was this baby in her arms.

It was, as I say, the kings
that caught us unawares . . .
Women have babies every other day,
not that we are there –
let's call it a common occurrence though,
giving birth. But kings
appearing in a stable with a
'Is this the place?' and kneeling,
each with his gift held out towards the child!

They didn't even notice us.
Their robes trailed on the floor,
rich, lined robes that money couldn't buy.
What must this child be
to bring kings from distant lands
with costly incense and gold?
What could a tiny baby make of that?

And what were we to make of it
was it angels falling through the air,
entwined and falling as if from the rafters
to where the gaze of the kings met the child's
– assuming the child could see?
What would the mother do with the gift?
What would become of the child?
And we'll never admit there are angels
or that somewhere between
one man's eyes and another's
is a holy place, a space where a king could be
at one with a naked child,
at one with an astonished soldier.

Christopher Pilling

Balthasar

'A cold coming we had of it'
('Journey of the Magi', T. S. Eliot)

Yes. It was cold. Of course. Specially the nights.
But we had furs and tents, good fires and lights.
The camel-men were unruly – but they always are;
You couldn't really complain. And that fantastic
    star
Impressed even them. Melchior kept on about the
    cold,
But he wasn't well, and face it, he was too old
For such a journey. For Caspar and me though, I'd
    say
It was a true adventure! So exciting! A great day
For astrology too! Just as we'd predicted.
    Everything!
Time. Place, Birth, Animals. It's true. The King
Wasn't quite what we'd thought, a bit of a
    disappointment.
But we left our gifts, the gold, the herbs, the
    ointment,

Made our speeches. The mother didn't seem too
    amazed,
Seemed to have expected us. – And no. It hasn't
    raised
The profile of astrology. A good thirty years have
    passed
And what with these Jerusalem riots, all that has
    got lost.
But I shan't forget the absolute delight
Of that strange journey. And we were all three
    quite
Certain something world-changing had happened
    that night.

Gerard Benson

BC:AD

This was the moment when Before
Turned into After, and the future's
Uninvented timekeepers presented arms.

This was the moment when nothing
Happened. Only dull peace
Sprawled boringly over the earth.

This was the moment when even energetic Romans
Could find nothing better to do
Than counting heads in remote provinces.

And this was the moment
When a few farm workers and three
Members of an obscure Persian sect

Walked haphazard by starlight straight
Into the kingdom of heaven.

U. A. Fanthorpe

I Never Trusted Herod

With his bright beady eye
With his slippery pink smile
And his, 'See you bye and bye . . .'
I never trusted Herod,
So why, oh why,
Did I tell him what I knew
Of the star in the sky?
I never trusted Herod
With his hand on my arm
Promising he meant the best
Saying 'There's no harm . . .'
I never trusted Herod
But I blabbed just the same
Shot my mouth off, said too much
And so I feel to blame
For what happened – for the soldiers,
When finally they came . . . $\longrightarrow$

I dream a lot of Herod
I dream we never met,
And all those little children
Are happy – living yet.
In my dreams the snow shines white.
The ice does not melt red
But when I wake I find
That still the dead are dead.

And the baby? Did he find him?
We left so fast – I never knew.
The baby underneath the star,
Did they kill him too?

Jan Dean

Innocent's Song

Who's that knocking on the window,
Who's that standing at the door,
What are all those presents
Lying on the kitchen floor?

Who is the smiling stranger
With hair as white as gin,
What is he doing with the children
And who could have let him in?

Why has he rubies on his fingers,
A cold, cold crown on his head,
Why, when he caws his carol,
Does the salty snow run red?

Why does he ferry my fireside
As a spider on a thread,
His fingers made of fuses
And his tongue of gingerbread? $\longrightarrow$

Why does the world before him
Melt in a million suns,
Why do his yellow, yearning eyes
Burn like saffron buns?

Watch where he comes walking
Out of the Christmas flame,
Dancing, double-talking:

Herod is his name.

Charles Causley

Flight into Egypt
(from an Italian painting
by Fra Angelico)

How should I guess
what I was carrying?
So human was the weight
held by his mother
in her cloak and wrappings –
a woman, delicate
after the birth.
How could I tell its value,
or dare to estimate?

I went soft-footed,
for the ground was sodden
with broken mud, sheep droppings,
mist, and snow . . .
A strange time to set out
on such a journey –
and where?
To what extremes?
I did not know. $\longrightarrow$

I have thought since:
why, after kings and angels
did they not travel
more like royalty?
But there was no one with us:
just a fellow
twitching the rein,
Mary, the child,
and me.

So we proceeded
through a different country,
moving by ways
I had not learned before.
It was hard going . . .
neither path nor compass
to lead us . . .
only light
from the heart's core.

Jean Kenward

The New Year

I am the little New Year, ho, ho!
Here I come tripping it over the snow.
Shaking my bells with a merry din –
So open your doors and let me in!

Presents I bring for each and all –
Big folks, little folks, short and tall;
Each one from me a treasure may win –
So open your doors and let me in!

Some shall have silver and some shall have gold,
Some shall have new clothes and some shall have
    old;
Some shall have brass and some shall have tin –
So open your doors and let me in!

Some shall have water and some shall have milk,
Some shall have satin and some shall have silk!
But each from me a present may win –
So open your doors and let me in!

Anon.

Good Riddance But Now What?

Come, children, gather round my knee;
Something is about to be.

Tonight's December thirty-first,
Something is about to burst.

The clock is crouching, dark and small,
Like a time bomb in the hall.

Hark! It's midnight, children dear.
Duck! Here comes another year.

Ogden Nash

New Year's Day Song

Walking by the river
on a chilly New Year's Day;
the wind cuts through the swaying grass,
a bitter wind at play.

High above the white-skinned trees
the crow squawks fill the air,
deep below the glassy ice
the river's bed is bare.

Walking by the river
on a chilly New Year's Day;
our breath as full as woodsmoke,
moisty whiteness turns to grey.

The trees that stand as sentries
salute the sinking sun,
the branches droop, the church bells chime,
they say Old Year is done, done, done.

John Rice

Promise

Remember, the time of year
when the future appears
like a blank sheet of paper
a clean calendar, a new chance.
On thick white snow

you vow fresh footprints
then watch them go
with the wind's hearty gust.
Fill your glass. Here's tae us. Promises
made to be broken, made to last.

Jackie Kay

Index of First Lines

Index of Poets

Acknowledgements

The publishers wish to thank the following for permission to use copyright material:

Gerard Benson: 'Balthasar', reprinted by permission of the author; **John Betjeman**: 'Christmas' from *Collected Poems*, reprinted by permission of John Murray (Publishers) Ltd; **Clare Bevan**: 'Just Doing My Job' and 'Listen', reprinted by permission of the author; **Stephen Bowkett**: 'Christmas Morning', reprinted by permission of the author; **Liz Brownlee**: 'Christmas Eve', reprinted by permission of the author; **Dave Calder**: 'Tree', 'We Are Not Alone', 'Stocking' and 'On the Thirteenth Day of Christmas My True Love Phoned Me Up . . .', reprinted by permission of the author; **Charles Causley**: 'The Reverend Sabine Baring-Gould' and 'Innocent's Song' from *Collected Poems for Children*, Macmillan Children's Books, and 'Mary's Song' from *The Gift of a Lamb*, Robson Books. Reprinted by permission of David Higham Associates Ltd; **Leonard Clark**: 'Bells Ringing' from *Singing in the Street*, published by Dennis Dobson; **Wendy Cope**: 'This Christmas Life' from *If I Know*, reprinted by permission of Faber and Faber Ltd; **John Cotton**: 'A Week to Christmas', reprinted by permission of the author; **Sue Cowling**: 'Wanted', reprinted by permission of the author; **Jan Dean**: 'Angels', 'Nativity' and 'I Never Trusted Herod' from *Wallpapering the Cat* published by Macmillan Children's

Books, reprinted by permission of the author; **T. S. Eliot**: 'Journey of the Magi' from *Collected Poems 1909–1962*, reprinted by permission of Faber and Faber Ltd; **U. A. Fanthorpe**: 'Reindeer Report', 'What the Donkey Saw' and 'BC:AD' from *Poems for Christmas* by The Peterloo Poets, reprinted by permission of the author; **Eleanor Farjeon**: 'In The Week When Christmas Comes' and 'Mary's Burden' from *Come Christmas*, and 'Christmas Stocking' from *Blackbird Has Spoken* published by Macmillan Children's Books. Reprinted by permission of David Higham Associates Ltd; **Eric Finney**: 'Robin', reprinted by permission of the author; **Mike Harding**: 'Christmas Market' and 'fr xmas' txt msg', reprinted by permission of the author; **Maureen Haselhurst**: 'Christmas at Four Winds Farm', reprinted by permission of the author; **Ted Hughes**: 'Snow and Snow', reprinted by permission of Faber and Faber Ltd; **Jackie Kay**: 'Promise', reprinted by permission of the author; **Jean Kenward**: 'Forecasts' and 'Flight into Egypt', reprinted by permission of the author; **John Kitching**: 'Red-berried Holly' and 'Bright Star', reprinted by permission of the author; **Patricia Leighton**: 'One Christmas Wish?', 'Thomas's First Christingle' and 'Nativity', reprinted by permission of the author; **Wes Magee**: 'The Christmas Shed', reprinted by permission of the author; **Ogden Nash**: 'Good Riddance But Now What?' from *Candy is Dandy: The Best of Ogden Nash*, by permission of André Deutsch Ltd; **David Orme**: 'A Martian Christmas', reprinted by permission of the author; **Gareth Owen**: 'Saturday

Night at the Bethlehem Arms', reprinted by permission of the author; **Brian Patten**: 'First Snow in the Street', reprinted by permission of Rogers, Coleridge & White on behalf of the author; **Christopher Pilling**: 'The Meeting Place' from *Poems for Christmas* published by The Peterloo Poets, reprinted by permission of the author; **John Rice**: 'New Year's Day Song', reprinted by permission of the author; **Coral Rumble**: 'Street Lights' and 'In a Forest Clearing', reprinted by permission of the author; **Roger Stevens**: 'Christmas Eve', reprinted by permission of the author; **Marian Swinger**: 'Little Donkey', 'The Innkeeper of Bethlehem' and 'The First Christmas', reprinted by permission of the author; **Alison Uttley**: 'Holly Red and Mistletoe White' from *Little Grey Rabbit's Christmas*, reprinted by permission of HarperCollins Ltd; **Philip Waddell**: 'The Christmas Eve News', reprinted by permission of the author.

Every effort has been made to trace the ownership of every selection included and to make full acknowledgement for its use. If any errors have accidentally occurred, they will be corrected in subsequent editions, provided notification is sent to the publishers.

THE
TRUTH
ABOUT
CHRISTMAS

PHILIP
ARDAGH

HAVE YOU EVER WONDERED?

Who decided to celebrate Christ's birthday on 25 December?
Why we kiss under the mistletoe?
Where the flying reindeer came from?
When the first Christmas card was sent?
What on earth a yule log has to do with Christmas?
What all that holly and ivy is for?
Why Christmas pudding is Christmas-pudding shaped?

★

The answers to these and many other festive questions are
packed within the covers of this gorgeous book.

What Are We Fighting For?

BRIAN MOSES AND ROGER STEVENS

Fascinating and moving in equal measure, this brand-new collection of poetry from Brian Moses and Roger Stevens explores the topic of war in a brilliantly accessible way for younger readers.

Find out about incredibly brave animals on the battlefield, the day soldiers played football in no-man's-land, poems about rationing and what it was like to be an evacuee, plus poems about the idea of warfare, asking the question What Are We Fighting For?

NEW POEMS ABOUT WAR